the art of getting by

chris mc geown

chris mc geown

other books by chris mc geown

dead of night (2017)

the man on the moon (2018)

the art of getting by

Copyright © 2019 Chris Mc Geown
All rights reserved.
ISBN: 9781730756658

CONTENTS

acknowledgments	i–v
long days	1–60
broken hearts	60–120
quiet nights	120-180
fresh starts	180-240

the art of getting by

to anyone reading this who may be struggling—i wish you courage, good luck, and a sense of humour

you will make it through

you will be okay.

long days

'there are still many more days of failure ahead, whole seasons of failure, things will go terribly wrong, you will have huge disappointments, but you have to prepare for that, you have to expect it and be resolute and follow your own path.'

—anton chekhov

the art of getting by

heavy hearts

come to me
heart in hands,
and i will hold it
while you heal.

stay gold

there are enough people
who will walk away
find the ones
that stay.

stagnant

i feel like i've aged
against my will
beyond my best before date,
every feeling a hollow version
of one i've felt before.

evolution

find the sun inside you,
and the rain will come—
and growth
will become
inevitable.

the art of caring

you do not need to
pick the flowers
to make them yours–
help them grow,
and you will forever
be a part of them.

chris mc geown

scorched earth

when you left
you left no memories untainted;
nothing grows here anymore
and nothing ever will.

attraction

i was mesmerized
when i saw you dancing
through the flames;
angel
or devil
the difference
was lost on me.

let it burn

i made the mistake
of self-destructing
just to see
if you cared.

oasis

life is easy
so damn simple
until it's not—

you feel the weight of the day
you feel the people look past you
look through you—

you feel the people walk past you
walk through you—

everything always comes easy
until you start to look for it—

the city can be a cold place,
so many people—
so much loneliness—

water, water everywhere, not a drop to drink.

daydreamers

to the 'crazy ones'
with the wild hearts
don't give up on the beauty
you are trying
to create.

sunrise/sunset

the stars come out
as the sun sets
and we find
beauty
in the little things
when the big things
disappear.

chilled to the bone

where are you?
i can't see you any more
but i can feel you
like the remnants of a winter breeze,
that chills you till you're cold
and leaves you shaking—
remember the warm summers?
where we laid on the beach
and then in bed?
it was never supposed to end
like this.

the art of letting go

sometimes you don't
fully appreciate someone's
presence,
until you feel
the weight of their absence—
the tragedy being,
that sometimes
it's too late.

born of fire

she had a heart of fire
reduced to ashes
her only romance
the changing winds.

world of pain

in the pain
of everything
i couldn't tell
if i was breaking
or becoming.

healing

do not fall for the ones
who will blame you for bleeding,
find the ones
that will help you
to heal.

sunflowers

that's the thing
about walls—
we build them so high
to protect ourselves—
but what happens
when we can't see the sun?

spirit of jazz

from the beginning
i knew
she was different—
she didn't just have
beauty
she had
soul.

tender hearts

love doesn't avoid the bad,
the dark places
in your mind—
love keeps you company,
love holds your hand,
love is gentle
when you are most fragile.

such great heights

peace comes
with perspective,
as all water
looks still
from a distance.

gasoline

like gasoline
helpless to the flame—
to blame me for burning
is to blame me for being—
sometimes things
simply demand
to be felt.

blood rush

her presence
never made me feel safe—
but it made me feel
so damn
alive.

the art of getting by

open

i no longer wish to be whole
but to be open
and grow
with reckless
abandon.

firefly

we are moulded
by fire—
but it's our form
not the flames
that define us.

far away

every man
wanted to feel
her beauty,
but none
would share
her pain.

waves

at night
her soul would dance
with the mesmerizing grace,
and unpredictable beauty
of the sea.

the art of getting by

jump

the fall was worth
every second
of flight.

just skin

bathed in moonlight
skin meets skin,
our souls dance
and dare
to dream
of love.

closest of calls

i don't know where my soul
should go,
i am made of many countries
but i don't know which is home,
i am everywhere
and nowhere—
a makeshift person
who was thrown together
into an improbable existence
one which i was not ready for—
each strand of DNA overcoming
a close call with death—
mine 3 pills deep trying to escape
losing myself in the process
sweating—
water
breathe
water
breathe—
i see my name in a small square of the newspaper,
i see my family crying,
i see the world spin on without me—
water
breathe
water

breathe—
the room comes back
my heart beats fast—
and i am lost
reborn
at rock bottom.

depression

there is no worse
sickness
than the sadness
of soul.

too close

her heart was restless—
it had been broken
enough times
to know
it is dangerous
to stay
in one place
for too long.

recovery

i'm sorry
i let you down,
but i had to
save
myself.

fragile

sometimes
we are afraid
that if we open up
we will fall
apart.

love conquers all

perhaps i was a fool
i waited for you every single night
for a call
or a text-
anything-
just hoping
every 'i love you'
was true.

lost

when we touch
i lose myself
in the loveliest
way.

lasting impression

i can no longer taste your lips
or see your smile
but i can still feel
every scar
you left.

peaks and valleys

our failures lead us
by pain
not pleasure—
but they still
move us
forward
in the end.

courage

there is nothing more courageous
than the heart that has been broken
over and over
with the courage to open
once more.

everyday people

do not be surprised
when men
without the patience
to understand you
do not have
the ability
to love you.

simple beauty

she has the beauty
of a universe
whose stars shine
for everyone
and no one
at all.

not your fault

it is unfair
to blame yourself
for the ways
that others
have let you down.

fiery

so many men
were drawn to her
warmth
but few could handle
the flames
within.

rose garden

there is nothing
more beautiful
than watching
flowers bloom
from the places
you bled.

summer sky

you saw my soul—
scars like stars
in the summer sky-
tracing constellations,
helping me find
my way home.

fate

the bird
born
nested in the branches,
realizes it has one of two fates—
to fall
or to fly.

wait

we were lost
when we found each other,
just two souls
dancing differently
to the same beat.

the wisdom of the plants

sometimes
the best way
to overcome a situation
is to grow
beyond it.

moving on

your scars
are a sign of strength
not weakness—
for many bleed
but few
truly
heal.

starlight

she was tired
of men
that fell in love
with their hands,
when there were stars
that bloomed
from her soul.

millennial ruining marriage

marriage is a term which scares me
almost as much as the word divorce—
remember the breaking of families
and forming of new ones
we had to 'try' and fit into—
new parents whose love was not unconditional
where we learned nothing gold can stay
and we were not enough
to make everyone happy—
the generation of divorce
waiting to be certain
in a world where nothing
ever is.

courage to feel

my heart breaks
for the men
that are too strong
to be sad,
who are pulled apart
at the seams
by their pride.

holding on

there is a difference
between leaving
and letting go.

flower child

she was just a girl
too beautiful for this world,
fighting fire
with flowers.

the art of getting by

when you left

i wished
to get so lost
that the suffering
would never
find me.

down

some days
the mask
doesn't help
some days
you just
sink.

ageing

the body
stretches and cracks
trying to contain
the beauty
that blossoms
within.

needs

when you feel bad
about the people who've left
ask yourself,
what kind of gardener
leaves
when the flower
starts to wilt?

broken hearts

'it is strange how often a heart must be broken
before the years can make it wise'

—sara teasdale

chris mc geown

the cold night sky

i felt like a fool—
you were my sun
while i was barely
a star
in your sky.

restless hearts

she had wild
in her eyes
to mask the sadness
in her soul.

the blues

what a beautiful
and dangerous thing it is
to care so deeply
it touches
your soul.

deepest wounds

i cannot promise
to heal you,
but i can promise
i will love you
deeper
than your deepest wound.

taking it to heart

that's the thing about wounds,
no matter where the knife went in
the blood
always comes
from the heart.

total darkness

i felt the kind of lost
you only feel
when the light
at the end of the tunnel
goes out.

asking for help

i remember
when i started
getting bad
like really bad
like unable to function in normal society bad,
like anxiety attacks every time i left the house bad,
like University grades going down faster than a meteor
that has just entered the atmosphere and discovered
gravity because i couldn't focus in class bad,
i decided to reach out for help—
i went to see a school therapist
and waited nervously to be called up
to finally tell someone about my problems
finally feeling some semblance of hope
but when i got to the desk
the stern woman who looked me up and down
and told me that waiting list to see someone
was 6 months,
so feeling rejected and unimportant i told her not to bother,
and i scrounged up money
for 3 sessions and $100 of help
with a women who could never quite
remember what we discussed

the art of getting by

the week before
and i decided it would be easier
to be 'okay'
and managed to white knuckle it well
until i graduated
and it got bad again—
like unable to get out of bed bad,
like staring at the subway wondering how bad things had to get to get the courage to jump bad—
and so i went to the government counselling office
and a stern woman looked me up and down,
and told me that their waiting list
was a year—
and it got worse
it got to the point where i felt like any help i asked for didn't matter
like i had to get worse to get help—
a game of chicken school and society
don't mind playing
as long as they have beautiful buildings
and nice things—
a flaw in a system where decisions are made by people with too much money and too good of therapists to know—
people who look after too many other people
to care,

and with some help from family and friends i somehow made it through,
but so many don't.

cold front

it was winter
in her soul
but she wore summer
on her lips—
the most dangerous storm
was brewing
inside of her.

wanting, waiting

it took me too long to realize
that no matter how much you love someone,
how hard you love them,
or how many thoughts
and sleepless nights
you give to them—
you can't make them
love you
back.

slow hands

you brushed your cold hands
over delicate skin—
every scar
was a story
you didn't care
to read.

painkiller

you said
my love
was a drug
that stopped
working.

yesterday

it was so hard
to let go
of my yesterdays
when that was
the only place
you lived.

chris mc geown

slow motion

there is no night lonelier
then the first
with a broken heart.

heartbeat

i have learned
to love
this body
which has held
together
my broken pieces
so beautifully.

denial twist

it was tough,
i didn't want the future
but rather some version of the past—
time moved forward
while i was lost
between past
and present.

indulgence

too often
we run
from the pain
of healing
to the pleasures
that destroy us.

falling to pieces

i held on so tight
when i should've let go
and it slowly
broke
both of us.

disoriented

i lost you
now every road
that was supposed to lead me
back home
only leaves me
more lost—
familiar roads
seem foreign
and nothing seems to make sense.

searching for you

in the darkness
i tried to find you
as my soul
got further
from the light.

distracted dream

i've spent my time
on a distracted planet
we put trees in money
and sell pieces of ourselves
to get it
and i wonder
if i am planting
my roots
in the wrong
place.

reconstruction

the best people i know
have had broken hearts
that they built up
better.

stranger than fiction

i wonder
how many times
you lied
when you said
you loved me—
i wonder
when it stopped being
true.

unbecoming

i never feel good enough–
even for the bad situations—
so i never know
when to walk
away.

untamed

she was never crazy—
she was wild,
and he
was weak.

endure

surviving the bad times
is the first step
to becoming
something better.

madness

you've crossed my mind
so many times
after midnight
it would be impossible to count—
haunting the place
you once called
home.

my head begs you to leave
but my heart calls you back
and i am at war
with myself.

late night conversations

she had
shared her bed
before,
but with him
she shared the stars.

dispensable

i was sad when you left
but i broke
when i realized
i was so easily
replaced.

i'm ready, i am

i am not this last year—
i am not a sum total of my mistakes,
many and recent,
but the lessons i have taken
from them—
my heart has been heavy
and hurting,
but i'm ready
to let go.

lost coastlines

i would not want
to contain an ocean
to a body
and call it love—
but rather bathe
in its beauty
and be free.

creature fear

consumed by the darkness
i feared the light,
that it might expose
the cracks
in my sinking ship.

impact

clipped wings,
her first lesson
in flight
was falling.

a cold goodbye

'what's it like losing someone
like that"

'like watching the sun
set
forever'.

broken record

you dressed my wounds
that you caused-
and told me it would be okay-
and i believed you
every
single
time.

soul

her love was
the night sky
on which my whole
universe
was painted.

real love

i don't want it to be easy
i want it to be real.

marathon

from morning to night
there was no rest
from the weight
i carried
and it broke me.

despair

have you ever missed someone
so much
you'd lose yourself
just to find them?

sweet nothing

you had me convinced
that if i didn't matter
to you
i wouldn't matter
at all.

paradise lost

it's hell
to call heartbreak
home.

sorrow

i am aged
by the memories
i've tried
so hard
to forget.

the art of getting by

carry on

there is courage
in every beat
of a broken
heart.

losing you

i love with my whole heart
or not at all–
i didn't lose a part of me,
i lost my whole damn self.

the art of getting by

don't let them see you cry

i didn't want you to see me
hurting—
i didn't want you to know
i still cared.

chaotic beauty

the men
who can't stand
to brave your storms
do not deserve
to bathe
in your beauty.

still life

i was lost
in the language
of her body—
the beauty i could feel
and longed
to understand.

free fall

it's hard to focus
on the horizon
when the ground
disappears
from beneath you.

unrequited

meaning will never
be found
in loving someone
who doesn't value
your presence.

patchwork

when you left
i found pieces of you
in the people i met,
but never the ones
that i needed
to patch the holes
in my broken heart.

ghosting

i sat
trying to figure out
how to mourn the loss
of someone
who still exists.

the sound of silence

listen to the silence
and find the truth
between what is said
and what is felt.

found

when you find someone
who turns being lost
into an adventure,
you are found—
you are home.

away

you look at me
with absent eyes
and i wonder
where
you've gone.

once more

i wished to see you
once more
and drown myself in your presence
so i wouldn't miss you
so damn much.

chris mc geown

empty

it was only supposed
to be a
broken heart–
why can i feel it
in my
soul?

my promise to you

just keep breathing
and i promise
the pain will pass
and the wounds will heal.

hanging on

it takes courage
to persist
when hope
is all
you have.

quiet nights

'when they were gone, she found her time hung heavy upon her hands'

—charlotte lennox

post-trauma

i escaped the pain
but the fear
never left.

hindsight

i think of everything
that you've done to me
and the best thing
that you did
was leave.

chris mc geown

i am

i am flawed,
i am whole,
i am beautiful.

heartless

how many times
can they break
your heart
until there's nothing left
to come back to.

chris mc geown

life

it is not selfish
to water your own garden
first.

this too (shall pass)

chase the sunlight
and the storm will follow–
but be still
and the storm
will pass.

bonfire

a bonfire burned out
by morning,
twisting the night away—
only the moon
knows
how brightly
we burned.

my love

you are a diamond;
delicate in appearance
unbreakable in existence.

old friend

i talk about
my depression
as though i have conquered it—
as though it is in the past—
as though it does not lurk
down inside of me
and call my name
at night.

the nature of beauty

sand slips
through fingertips—
the futile grasping
and fleeting beauty,
as it returns
to where it belongs.

soulmate

when i see you
i am convinced
that there is no death
that wouldn't make life
worth living.

sight unseen

i avoid your eyes
and act indifferent
because if you saw my soul
you might see me
falling apart.

the numbness

the problem is
you can't just numb
the pain
without losing feeling
everywhere.

her

she had been hurt so much
and yet still she continued on
some would call her a fool
but she is the bravest person
i know.

silence

when i moved to the UK,
i wasn't sure what to expect—
it's a small neighbourhood
smaller apartment,
a new slum
of the old and the new
an old building
with new fixtures
that don't work together
but somehow still coexist—
i don't mind it here—
there is a calm in the night around 1 am
only broken, sometimes,
by a baby crying
then a man yelling
and then a woman yelling back—
the man resents the woman
and the woman resents the man for resenting her—
the baby knows no better,
but is slowly learning—
the people here are okay though
for the most part
until they drink too much
and remember
that they are not okay—

but when the silence finally hits
it is deafening—
the siren songs of settling
when the city goes to sleep.

eternal

she's got a smile
that makes me think
all my past lives
were spent
with her.

still learning

learn
to sit comfortably
in your skin
learn
to spend less time wishing
and more time dreaming
learn
that nothing
is as serious
as it seems
at the time,
and that the first breath
after your heart breaks
is the hardest but the most important—
learn
to accept love
and let go of poison people—
learn to be better to yourself.

exposed

vulnerable
with the sting
of fresh air
to old wounds
hoping
they will finally
heal.

one more time

at such a late hour
rationality abandons me
and my heart screams out for you—
and i would bear the pain
of losing you again,
just to see you
once more.

longing

the fear carved
in longing and in
letting myself down
time after time—
ruining a good thing
because i didn't feel worthy
to have it.

better left unsaid

i can't explain
why when my mind wanders
it's always
to you.

wake

after all that's happened
the hardest thing
isn't watching people go
it's letting people in.

sweet embrace

insecurities
embraced,
not overlooked–
beasts
tamed
by the power
of love.

give me stitches

be soft enough
to accept the pain
of the needle and thread—
this is the beginning
of healing.

old haunts

once you've found home
in a heart
it makes it hard
to let go.

a conversation with my mom about a photo

she hung a picture on the wall,
she hung a picture on the wall from after a visit to her grandma's house,
she hung a picture on the wall from after a visit to her grandma's house and she was six,
she hung a picture on the wall from after a visit to her grandma's house and she was six and looked miserable,
it took me a while to notice that she hung this picture on the wall from after a visit to her grandma's house and she was six and looked miserable,
when i notice i asked her 'why did you hang a picture on the wall from after a visit to your grandma's house when you were six and looked miserable?',
and she told me she hung a picture on the wall from after a visit to her grandma's house and she was six and looked miserable because she had been sexually assaulted by her uncle that day and many times before and after it was taken,
and so i asked her 'why in the world would you hang a picture on the wall from after a visit to your grandma's house when you were six and looked miserable because you had been sexually assaulted by your uncle that day and many times before and after.'
she said it was to remind her that she was only young

when it happened, that it was not her fault, and that she deserved better—
and in that moment i realized the man had not only taken her innocence, but made her carry the weight of the guilt for many years—and i could think of no worse thing—
so i hugged my mom,
and i cried at her strength.

eye of the storm

it was chaos keeping me
together
until i fell apart
in silence.

boxer

it took me too long
to realize
love is not
a war to be won
but a dance
to be shared.

chris mc geown

deep water

we are the ones
who know
that the deepest wounds
are caused
by the closest hands.

scars

i speak in generalities
and cliches-
i show you the skin
while the scars reach
for my bones.

breaking point

sometimes
the pain
of trying
to hold yourself together
is worse
than allowing yourself
to fall apart.

wildfire

drawn to the warmth
you moved through me
like wildfire–
the beautiful
dance
of destruction.

echo

the universe you project
is nothing
but a reflection
of the beauty
inside.

together

you are not some fragile flower—
we plant the garden together
and we share the beauty
that grows.

simple truth

when skin meets skin
and two souls dance
nothing else
should matter.

looking glass

she had a love
that could see
beyond the words
to see
what's in
your soul.

stranger

i had been wearing the mask
for so long
i forgot
who i was
beneath it.

civil twilight

i crave a romance
like the sea
and the setting
sun.

last call

you were stuck
trying to dress a wound
you couldn't find
but always feel—
trying to drown the pain with alcohol—
all your demons
swimming
inside of you.

freedom

cut by the pieces
of my broken heart,
i realized
it was time
to let go.

time

it is no coincidence
that through the longest days
and lonely nights
we grow
the most.

sleeping sickness

you came back—
now i spend my nights
wondering
if you are in love
or just scared
of being
alone.

sweet surrender

she had a way
of quieting
the parts of me
that wished
i was someone
else.

tender is the night

in the midst of the chaos
i closed my eyes
and watched the stars bloom slowly
through the darkness-
and in this moment
i knew
i would be okay.

damaged

i'm sorry
for all my mistakes-
good love
was a language
i had
to learn.

permanent hesitation

i feel apprehensive
because i know
that even the cruel hand
is kind
at first.

chris mc geown

when seasons change

i don't know what's going on
inside of me-
the roses of summer have gone
and all i am left with
are thorns.

nothing left

forgive my madness—
but i lost everything
before i lost myself.

resolve

tonight
i decided
i'm done spending time
with ghost and souls
of loves
who've left.

anxiety

do you know
how it feels
to be constantly
creating
contingency plans
because you never
feel good enough
for the moment?

past in pieces

since you left
the night is broken—
a kaleidoscope
of visions from a past life
that keep me up
til dawn.

skin & bones

the heart wants
what it wants—
ignore it
and it consumes you
until you are nothing
but skin
and bones.

beyond reason

i followed my heart
to the edge
of reason
and almost lost my mind
in the process.

skinny love

if your words
meant nothing
then who the hell was i
and what
did i mean
to you?

fairytale

i was told to be perfect—
breaking from the pressure—
waiting on some fairytale version of me
to save me from myself,
slowly self-destructing,
just wondering
when they will come.

lucid

there are memories so vivid
i wish i could slip back in time
and bathe in the moment,
allowing it to consume me,
instead of the distant longing—
the visions of ghosts
that haunt me.

far

i caught myself in a distant dream—
with you and me,
and the people
we used
to be.

fresh starts

'the real voyage of discovery consists not in seeking new landscapes, but in having new eyes'

—marcel proust

handwritten

she wrote in ink on her skin
to remind her
that no matter how
they try and paint her
she is the canvas,
the artist,
the masterpiece.

done

the best revenge
is that i stopped caring
the moment
you left.

aching

pain is wisdom
waiting
to be realized.

bad breaks

some people aren't tough
because they want to be–
some people are tough
because they have to be.

in bloom

when i broke
i discovered
the beauty
i was holding
inside.

the art of getting by

two moons

i want to know
who gave you those scars–
who stole your sun,
and sewed the moon
into your skin–
i want to understand you,
and sit in the darkness with you
while our souls share the stars.

women

call me woman,
you will be mistaken—
for i am not worthy of the title
of the ones who give life-
the shapers,
the artists,
the creators
from which all life
blooms.

grace

her beauty
predisposed her
to disaster—
but what a beautiful
chaos
she created.

deepest sleep

i do not fear death—
for at night
i cease to exist
and when i wake
i miss the peace.

old wounds

deny the pain
and it will find you
on your darkest
nights.

unfair

people who use
your past
to tear you down
do not deserve
to be with you
in the present.

existence

to me
it has always been crazy—
people claiming land
and fighting wars,
instead of acknowledging
how crazy it is
to be anything
at all.

good morning

face bathed in sun
it's been so long
since i had a love
that lasted
till morning.

still standing

courage is knowing
you can stand on your own
and still be
strong.

behold the hurricane

when you left
i embraced the chaos—
the destruction
distracted me
which was better
than missing
you.

the art of getting by

breathe

i crave solitude
for when the weight of the world
and these walls
are too heavy
i can set them down
and breathe.

chris mc geown

walking wounded

sometimes
in this world
it is so easy
to bleed
and so hard
to ask
for help.

intuition

listen to the longing,
the restless soul
guides
through feeling.

distant beauty

i watched the stars
bloom from your soul
then sat
in awe
of the constellations.

comfortably numb

i sink deep
into my soul
where the echoes turn to silence
and the pain turns to numbness—
and for a minute
i am
okay.

hospice

the truth is
you can try and protect someone
but you cannot
save them
from themselves.

wild hearts

her heart
was always
as beautiful
as the sunset
and as restless
as the sea.

breaking the habit

sometimes
the best way
to break
the pattern
is to be still.

dear sweet disaster

some things
don't end neatly—
sometimes
it's about learning
when
to walk
away.

the simple truth about healing

take some time—
it's hard
to heal
when you're still
bleeding.

eternal glow

when you are feeling lonely
and full of self-doubt
i wish that i could show you
the way light shines from your soul
and all of the people
it touches.

worthy

you are worthy of love,
stop trying so hard
to find it—
just be
and let the love
find you.

just love

the pure heart
has no map
no country
no borders
no rules,
just love.

chris mc geown

war all the time

when the dust had settled
and i looked
at the destruction
i realized
that no war
is ever won.

distorted reflected

everything i was
and everything i wasn't
caught in a reflection
of a love
i had lost.

fearless

she wears fire
but she never fears
the flames.

push and pull

i was so scared to lose you
i craved a closeness
you could not give
pushing you away
in the process.

drunk on you

her soul
was as pure
as water
but it moved
through me
like wine.

the art of getting by

for real

sometimes
i am so thankful
for the bad times—
people left
and i fell apart,
but what i was left with
was real.

calling me home

lately
i've been longing
for something
i lost–
a touch i can't fully remember
but one
i can't bring myself
to forget.

becoming the hurricane

she became the storm—
now the only thing
she had to run from
was herself.

chris mc geown

weathering the storm

some days
you can't control
the waves
you can only try
and keep your head
above water.

the art of getting by

made

you tore me down
then built yourself
up
with my broken
pieces.

let them leave

love cannot be cornered,
love is not an ultimatum,
love does not need to be convinced to stay—
if someone wants to leave
let them.

star-crossed

star-crossed lovers
just so lucky
that for the moment
the universe
doesn't seem
so lonely.

the hard times

your absence said more
than your presence
ever could.

i've changed

somewhere inside me
was something you missed–
an empty field
full of seeds
that bloomed
when you left.

road regrets

oh what i would give
to have you near me
and hear your voice
fill the silence
once more.

wasted time

whether you receive love
or a lesson
the love you give
is never wasted.

addiction

when loving them
breaks you more
than leaving
it is time
to let
go.

seaside

like still waters
her quiet beauty
calms
my soul.

perfect stranger

that's the problem
reaching out for connection
from a dark place—
you're never sure
what reaches back.

let me go

you keep me hanging on
to this sinking ship—
let me go
let me drown
let me try and swim
on my own.

wildflower

she was never crazy
she was free
in a way
that most people
never understand.

onwards

i burned
my bridges—
i had no intentions
of going back
to something
that hurt me
so badly.

self

i am so thankful
for the hard times
that brought me closer
to myself.

saviour

instead of looking for someone
to save you
focus on becoming someone
who can save
themselves.

chris mc geown

a different kind of lonely

reduce her to her body
and miss the stars
that bloom
from her soul.

enigma

it's hard to explain
she is as soft
as the rain
but she sets
my soul
on fire.

lowest of the low

i couldn't tell
what was worse—
that you broke me—
or that i blamed myself
for breaking.

quiet beauty

it's not with pressure
but with patience
that the flower
blooms.

the art of getting by

you can't always
be fixed
but you can always
grow.

whole

it's so easy to idealize something you will never have
as the piece that makes you whole-
just one more purchase
just one more person,
while what you have
slips away.

(with you)

i'd love
for nothing more
than to find myself
lost
with you.

shadows of dawn

the only way
to get them
to stop haunting you
is to be kinder
to yourself.

chris mc geown

the ones who stay

she braved the chaos
in my head
to sit with my heart
and i hope she knows
how much
that means.

sun hands

your touch feels different,
tender hands
that plants seeds
from the places
where others
plucked flowers.

dependency

you said
no one could love me
more than you did.

and in that moment
i realized
i had to be better
to myself.

foundation

in patience
and stillness
there is a strength
that can withstand
any storm.

written in the stars

our fate not marked
by the stars
but in our scars
and the lessons
we learn
from them.

Made in the USA
Monee, IL
01 February 2025